The World's Harvest

METALS AND MINERALS

Jacqueline Dineen

ENSLOW PUBLISHERS, INC.
Bloy St & Ramsey Ave.
Box 777
Hillside, N.J. 07205

Metals and minerals are essential to our way of life. This is the story of how they are found, taken out of the ground, and put to use.

Contents

j553
D61m
C.1

	Introduction	3
1.	Where do minerals come from?	5
2.	Mining for minerals	10
3.	Using metals	16
4.	Precious metals and stones	24
5.	The future for minerals	30
	Index	32

The picture above shows a small part of a shallow diamond mine in South Africa.
[cover] The cover picture shows the gold death-mask of King Tutankhamun, which was gently hammered into shape over 3,000 years ago.
[title page] The picture on the title page shows the fierce heat of the coke ovens in an iron and steel works.
[1–23] All other pictures are identified by number in the text.

This series was developed for a worldwide market.

First American Edition, 1988
© Copyright 1987 Young Library Ltd
All rights reserved.
No part of this book may be reproduced by any means without the written permission of the publisher.

Printed in the United States of America

10 9 8 7 6 5 4 3 2 1

Library of Congress Cataloging-in-Publication Data

Dineen, Jacqueline.
  Metals and minerals.
  (The world's harvest)
  Includes index.
  Summary: Explains how man searches for minerals in the ground and how these minerals are mined and put to use.
  1. Metals--Juvenile literature. 2. Mines and mineral resources--Juvenile literature.
  [1. Metals. 2. Mines and mineral resources]
  I. Title. II. Series: Dineen, Jacqueline. World's harvest.
  TN148.D56 1988   553   88-1192
  ISBN 0-89490-218-0

Introduction

A mineral is anything which is not an animal or a plant. The two main kinds of minerals are stone and metals, and these are the kinds which are mined. If you ever see a mine, you may be sure it is something to do with minerals. The mine in picture [1] is a diamond mine in Namibia, but iron, coal, salt,

[1]

A geologist is a scientist who studies the earth and the rocks of which it is made.

and copper are all minerals too, and there are many more.

Can you imagine the world today without minerals? Aircraft, ships, trains, bridges, and machinery are made of metal. Roads and buildings are made of stone. Coal and uranium fuel power stations to give us light and heat. All these things are minerals.

In chapter 1 I tell you how metals and other minerals were discovered in primitive or ancient times. I describe some of the early metalworking, and how it led to modern methods of manufacture. In chapter 2 I tell you how geologists set about finding the minerals, and how mining companies get them out of the ground.

Iron and steel are the most used metals, so in chapter 3 I tell you how it is mined and how so many things are made from it. In chapter 4 I tell you something about precious metals and stones. 'Precious' means they are highly valued for their rarity and beauty, and not merely for the uses which we put them to. We see how gold and silver are mined and how they are used. I explain what diamonds and other precious stones look like when they come out of the mine, and how they are cut and polished to make sparkling jewels.

We are using minerals up very quickly, and they will not last for ever. In the last chapter I tell you how people are trying to save the metals we have and prevent waste. We are exploring for minerals under the sea and beneath the ice cap of Antarctica. In our modern age, we need more minerals than ever before.

1 · *Where do minerals come from?*

The earth is made up of rocks and other minerals. It has an outer layer of solid rock which is called the earth's crust. Inside this crust is the central core which is so hot that the rocks and other minerals there are a fiery boiling liquid.

Millions of years ago, the crust was very thin. There were many huge eruptions when volcanoes flung masses of the molten rock and metal to the surface, just as you can see in picture [2]. Earthquakes tore the crust apart, releasing more liquid metals and rocks. Some metals stayed on the surface; others were trapped some way below. They cooled and became solid as part of the crust.

[2]

Some metals and rocks were all mixed together and that is how they cooled and solidified. Rock and metal mixtures are called metallic ores. Other metals stayed separate from the rocks. These are called free metals.

Later in prehistory, the planet was cooled by torrential rains. These rains lasted for hundreds of years and caused more changes to the surface of the earth. Rivers and seas wore away the soil and rock. Tons of soil were washed on top of rocks and metals, burying them and forming new layers of rock on top.

Millions of years later Man arrived on the earth, and eventually discovered that some of the minerals could be useful. People hunted animals for food, and for this they needed weapons. The first weapons were made from stones and rocks. Later they learnt how to sharpen them to a deadly point.

Early discoveries and uses of metals

Among the stones the hunters used were metallic lumps like gold and copper. People realised that these metals were different. They could be bent and shaped without chipping and breaking. They had made an important discovery.

They also learned that some types of stone could be used for building, and that others were very beautiful and could be made into jewellery. They found that heavy clays could be moulded into shapes like cups and pots which set hard when they were fired at great heat.

Examples of metalwork have been found which date back to about 10,000 B.C. The picture on the cover shows the gold death-mask of King Tutankhamun, who lived in Egypt more than 3,000 years ago. This work was done by hammering the gold into the shape required. In picture [3] you can see some tools for working gold. They have not changed much since ancient times.

Gold is soft and can be shaped quite easily, but copper breaks if it is hammered too much. People were baffled by this problem for a long time. Then they discovered that if copper was hammered a bit, then heated in the fire, then hammered some more, it was far easier to work with. This process, which is called annealing, was a big step in the history of metalwork.

Up till now, people had only used free metals which they found lying around in streams or on the earth's surface. However, most metal is in the form of metallic ores, as I described above. So the next useful discovery was 'smelting', which is the process used to extract metal from rock.

Smelting requires rock to be heated to a great temperature so that the metal melts and runs out. No one is quite sure how this discovery was made, but perhaps in about 4,000 B.C. people were heating pottery in kilns made of rock. The rock had copper ore in it. As the kiln heated up, the copper melted and dripped out of the rock and collected in pools on the floor. This exciting discovery would have set people searching for more rocks with metal in them.

Over the next thousand years, people learnt more about finding and fashioning metals.

[3]

A kiln is a type of oven in which new-made pottery is hardened by baking.

[4] They also found new types such as silver, lead, and tin. Then it was discovered how to make 'alloys'. An alloy is a mixture of two or more types of metal to make a new man-made metal. The first alloy was bronze, which is a mixture of tin and copper.

So the history of metal progressed. The next metal to be found was iron. Iron is still one of the most important of all metals and new mines are being opened every year. The one in picture [4] is in Quebec in Canada.

Then came mercury and zinc, then pewter which is an alloy of tin and lead, and brass which is an alloy of zinc and copper. All the time people were developing new methods to create sharper and stronger weapons, and finer gold and silver articles. During the last two centuries many new metals have been discovered. Nickel, manganese, and aluminium are three important ones.

Today, minerals are even more valuable than they were hundreds of years ago. We use them in huge quantities, and would find it impossible to manage without them. What would we do without the machinery, vehicles, and tools made from metal, or the houses, roads, and dams made from stone? We would be like primitive people again.

Precious stones

There are other metals and stones which are not essential, but which make life more happy and beautiful. Jewellery is made from rare, precious stones like diamonds, rubies, emeralds, and sapphires. There are lovely semi-precious stones such as amethyst, topaz, and aquamarine.

These minerals are not just lying around waiting to be picked up. They have to be searched for, and some of them lie hundreds of metres below the surface of the earth. Mines have to be sunk to get at stocks of coal, salt, metals, and precious stones.

In the next chapter I tell you how the search begins.

2 · *Mining for minerals*

Before we begin mining, we have to be fairly sure where the minerals are. We do not just start digging anywhere and hope for the best. The first step is to know which sort of rocks the minerals might be in. Then we have to know where those rocks might be found. The search begins with the geologists.

In picture [5] you can see a geologist investigating a single slab of rock in her laboratory. Geologists study the history of rocks going back many hundreds of thousands of years, long before Man appeared on the earth. They discover how the seas and continents were formed into the shapes they are today. This knowledge helps them to work out what the world beneath our feet is made of. It is easy enough to see what is on the surface, but the geologists have to work out what is hundreds or even thousands of metres below.

The earth is a mass of rock stretching down to the central core, which is still hot and molten. We cannot reach most of this rock because we cannot drill far enough into the earth. All the materials we need are taken from the outer crust, which is over twenty kilometres thick under land and about ten kilometres thick under the oceans.

The crust is made up of many different types of rock and soil. You have probably noticed the different types just by looking around you, at a cliff face, or at the bare banks

[5]

[6]

of a river. Soil may be soft and fine like sand, or heavy and sticky like clay. Rock may be grey, or yellow, or red, or white; it may be impossible to break, or flaky, or so soft that you can grind it into a powder.

Some rocks, such as granite, were formed as the molten materials in the crust cooled down millions of years ago. These rocks hardened into crystals which were pushed together to form solid rock. Rocks of this type are called 'crystalline' or 'igneous' rock.

Other rocks were formed by rivers carrying mud and sand down from high ground and depositing it on lower ground and in the sea. As this heavy mound of silt built up, the lower layers were pressed more and more tightly together. They formed 'sedimentary' rocks such as sandstone and limestone.

Different types of rock are piled on top of one another in layers all the way through the earth's crust. The shallow diamond mine in picture [6] shows these layers clearly. Some of the layers are thick, and some are very thin. They do not always lie in neat horizontal stripes, but weave up and down and sometimes disappear altogether.

Various ways of surveying deep rocks

Gravity is the force which pulls everything towards the centre of the earth.

It is not enough for the geologists to know what there is near the surface, or in one small area. It might be very different a few metres away. So they carry out surveys of the rock layers. They can make aerial surveys which show them the layout of a whole area. They use instruments to help them find out about the layers below the surface. They can measure the magnetism in rocks and minerals with a magnetometer. The pull of gravity is stronger in some rocks which contain metal, and this can be measured with a gravimeter.

Geologists can also make a 'seismic' survey. A hole is drilled in the rocks and a small explosion is set off. They measure the time it takes the shockwaves from the various rocks to travel back to the surface. This helps to tell them how deep the rock layers are, what types of rocks there are, and whether they might contain metals.

When the geologists think there are valuable minerals deep in the earth, the mining company first makes a test drilling. A small drilling rig is set up, and the drill bores its way through the rock. The drill carries a hollow pipe with it into the ground. Further lengths of pipe are added as the drill goes deeper. When the drill is pulled up, the hollow pipes contain lengths of rock which show samples of all the different layers. These are called 'core' samples, and you can see one of them in picture [7].

If the core samples show that the rocks

[7]

contain valuable minerals, mining engineers decide how to get them out of the earth. Much depends on how deeply they are buried.

Some minerals are found very near the surface, and these can be recovered by opencast mining. Copper, diamonds, coal, gold, iron, and uranium are some of the minerals which are mined in this way. Huge excavators cut away the surface soil and rock, and lift out the ores. When an area has been mined thoroughly, the hole is often filled up again.

Quarries look a bit like opencast mines, but here the minerals being sought are not metals but stone. Building materials such as granite, chalk, sandstone, marble, slate, gravel, and sand are all taken from quarries.

If the minerals are deep in the ground, a vertical mine shaft must be sunk. Coal, rock salt, gold, silver, copper, lead, and zinc are often found very deep down. At the bottom of the shaft, miners tunnel sideways into the rock to cut out the valuable ores. This work used to be done with pick and shovel, but nowadays it is done with machines. In picture [8] South African miners are drilling a tunnel in a gold mine.

If the ore is not too far down, the engineers may decide on a drift mine. The entrance to a drift mine is a long sloping tunnel instead of a vertical shaft. The miners extend the tunnel as they cut out the ore.

Some minerals are taken from the sea. Salt, for example, is produced by evaporating sea water, then purifying the remaining solids to extract the salt.

[8]

[9]

All countries have some useful minerals. Some have a vast quantity. Most gold, silver, and copper are found in the United States, Africa, Canada, and Australia. The largest source of gold and diamonds is South Africa. Iron and lead are mined in many places, including the United States, Australia, Canada, South America, and parts of Europe. Uranium is found in Australia and the United States of America.

One of the more modern metals is aluminium. It is found in an ore called bauxite. Aluminium is one of the world's most plentiful metals, but no one could find an efficient way to separate the metal from the ore until the nineteenth century. One of its most useful qualities is its lightness. The aeroplane in picture [9] is made largely of aluminium, and so are other planes today.

3 · Using Metals

The broken rock in picture [10] is iron ore. Iron is the metal we use most today, but not in its basic form. If you look around you will probably see some things made of iron, but you will see a lot more made of steel. Steel is made from iron and carbon.

Iron is never found lying around in lumps. It is all buried in iron ores. Luckily for us, there is plenty of iron ore in the world. The ore is mined from opencast mines and exported to all the countries which need it. It is carried overland by train, and loaded on to huge ships which take it to its destination.

Before the iron can be used, it has to be separated from the ore. This was quite a

[10]

problem for early people. They had discovered the smelting process for metals such as copper, but they had not come across such a strong metal as iron. It was very difficult to get a fire hot enough to soften the iron at all. Early ironworkers made small furnaces and produced some spongy iron which could be hammered into shape. They burned charcoal in these furnaces and discovered that if some of the carbon from the charcoal got into the iron it made the iron stronger.

In the fifteenth century the first blast furnace was introduced in Germany. Blast furnaces were powered by water, and later by steam; they could produce far greater heat than anything thought of before. Huge bellows fanned the fire and increased the temperature; but still the iron did not melt completely. Neither charcoal nor coal produced enough heat to melt iron satisfactorily.

Charcoal is made from partly burned wood, and the forests could not provide enough. As the iron industry grew, the charcoal supply began to run out. In the eighteenth century, an Englishman called Abraham Darby began to experiment with turning coal into a fuel suitable for iron-making.

When coal burns it gives off a gas called sulphur. Darby discovered that if coal was burned in a closed oven, the sulphur was driven out. The fuel that remained was called coke.

Coke is still the fuel used in the iron and steel industry. On the title page is a picture of a coke oven. The oven heats up an enclosed tank called a furnace. Modern furnaces, like

A furnace is a gigantic enclosed oven which is capable of producing extreme heat.

[11]

the one in picture [11], are enormous and can stand tremendous heat. Blasts of air keep the coke burning at a ferocious rate. The heat is so intense that parts of the outside of the furnace have to be cooled with water so that they do not burn through. This heat melts the iron and other minerals in the ore until they are completely liquid.

The molten iron collects at the bottom of the furnace. What happens next depends on whether it is to be used for iron or steel. If it is to be used for iron, it runs out of the furnace into moulds, where it is allowed to set into solid blocks called 'pig iron'. In picture [12] you can see the molten iron, still glowing with heat, pouring out of the furnace into two long rows of moulds. In its set form it is called cast iron.

A mould is a hollow shape which is filled with molten metal. When the metal cools it sets into the shape of the mould.

[12]

Molten iron can be poured into other shapes of moulds to make various cast iron objects. These moulds are normally made in a special sand which is heat-resistant. Complicated pieces of machinery can be made in this way. So can hollow objects like pipes.

Cast iron is heavy and brittle, and it cannot be bent into shape without breaking. Steel is an easier metal to work with, so much of the iron that comes out of the furnace is turned to steel.

Iron for steel-making is kept molten in huge vessels called ladles. You can see it being poured into a ladle in picture [13]. These ladles are carried on rails or by overhead cranes to the steel-making furnaces.

The molten iron contains impurities which have to be removed to produce steel. This is what happens in a steel-making furnace. In the most widely used type, a jet of oxygen is blown in so that the furnace flares up and impurities are burnt away. This process is called a 'blow' and produces a pure steel.

Electric furnaces are used for special sorts of steel which are made by adding other metals to carefully selected steel scrap. Ordinary steel would rust if it came into contact with water too often. Nickel and chromium are added to make a steel which does not rust. This is called 'stainless steel'. The cutlery in your home is almost certainly made of stainless steel.

To prevent it rusting, steel can also be plated with tin. Tin cans are made in this way.

Steel can be shaped in various ways. It can be poured or 'cast' into moulds, like iron, but

[13]

[14]

this method is used only for special castings. Manufacturers often want to buy steel in sheets or other convenient forms which they can then shape for themselves.

When the molten steel comes out of the furnace it runs into huge moulds like the one in picture [14]. There it is allowed to cool into ingots. A steel ingot can weigh up to twenty tonnes. When it is solid, but not cold, it passes to the rolling mill to be made into sheets. The ingot is forced between rollers to the thickness required, rather like rolling out pastry. Picture [15] shows a section of a rolling mill.

The rolling process is used for making flat sheets, shaped pieces of steel like railway lines, and hollow articles like pipes. Special rolling machines are used to make different items. Steel wire is made by rolling and rolling the steel until it is very thin. It then goes on to a machine which has fine holes called dies. The wire is pulled through smaller and smaller holes until it is the right thickness.

Steel can also be shaped by continuous casting. In this method, the liquid steel is poured into a long, narrow chute, and as it passes through the chute it gradually cools. More liquid is continuously added at the top. The result is an endless rod of steel, molten at one end and solid at the other. The lower end can be cut into the lengths required before rolling. In this way there is no waste.

Solid steel objects such as large machine parts are made by a process called forging. The hot ingot is pressed into shape in a huge machine called a forging press. The first ironworkers hammering their softened metals

[15]

into shape would have found this machine very useful, because it is just a modern version of their technique. The top of the press, the 'hammer', is shaped to press out the article required against the bottom part, the 'anvil'.

Steel can be used in many ways, but it has one disadvantage which cannot be overcome. It is heavy. Aluminium, however, is a very light metal. It is found in an ore called bauxite, and people have known about it for thousands of years. The problem was that when the bauxite was removed, it left a substance called alumina. This is a mixture of aluminium and oxygen which is not workable.

For centuries people wrestled with the problem of how to separate the metal from the oxygen. At last, in 1886, it was achieved by use of an electric current, and suddenly aluminium was an everyday metal. Today it is used in hundreds of ways, from packaging food to building trains, aircraft, and ships.

Producing aluminium from bauxite

Bauxite is found in most continents of the world, but the best ore for alumina is mined in tropical and semi-tropical regions. The mines are opencast. The ore is taken to an alumina plant where the alumina is separated from the bauxite. Then the alumina is processed to separate the metal, at an aluminium plant.

Alumina is often exported in its raw state and made into aluminium in the country which buys it. The aluminium plant in picture [16], for example, is in Canada. Australia is the world's largest producer and exporter.

Pure aluminium is not very strong, but it

can be made much stronger by alloying with another metal called magnesium. This alloy is called duralumin.

Metals old and new

Several new metals have been discovered in the last century or so. Uranium is used to fuel nuclear power stations. Tungsten is a heavy metal which can withstand great heat, so it is used to make things like the tips of high-speed drills, electrical contacts, and the filaments in light bulbs.

Meanwhile, some of the earliest known metals are still very important to us. Copper is a good conductor of heat and is used to make pipes for hot water and central heating. Copper wire is used in many electrical appliances because electricity flows so well through it. Lead is used as a protective shield in nuclear power stations. Throwaway batteries are made from zinc. The liquid in the thermometer which tells you if you have a temperature is mercury.

4 · Precious metals and stones

The metals I told you about in the last chapter are the everyday metals which you see around you in cars, houses, railways, bridges, and a thousand other places. This chapter is about precious metals and stones. Gold, silver, and platinum are examples of precious metals. Diamonds, emeralds, and rubies are examples of precious stones.

Gold is the most precious of metals. The world's money system is based on the value of gold, and coins like those in picture [17] used to be made from it.

Gold can be found lying in rivers, or on the earth's surface, or deep in the ground. Some of the world's deepest gold mines are in South Africa. The gold is found in tiny flecks spread through sedimentary rocks. The ore has to be extracted and the gold separated from it. The deposits which are washed down by mountain streams may contain larger pieces of gold called 'nuggets'. Gold has also been found in veins in rock fairly near the surface, where it can be mined by opencast methods. It is so rare and valuable that no piece is too small to be worth extracting.

A country's wealth is measured by the amount of its gold reserves. The pile shown in picture [18] is worth more than the whole economy of some small countries.

Gold is a heavy, soft metal which can be shaped into beautiful ornaments and jewellery. A thin layer of it—called gold plate—can be

[17]

A nation's gold reserve is the total amount of gold in coins and bars held by the government. It maintains the value of the paper notes and coins which the government issues as money.

[18]

used to cover other metals. However, gold is not an exotic metal only. It also has some industrial uses.

It does not rust or tarnish, as copper does, so electrical contacts which are exposed to the weather are covered with gold plate. A thin layer of gold reflects the heat from the engines of powerful jet aircraft and prevents the bodywork from melting. Dental fillings for your teeth may be made with gold alloys, and some people have broken teeth capped with gold.

Silver, not nearly so expensive as gold, has been used for making jewellery for thousands of years. It is often found in large nuggets, though most of the world's silver comes from ores which are mined in Australia, the United States, Canada, Burma, and parts of South America. It can be polished to a fine lustre, but it tarnishes if it is not kept clean. Silver is used to make jewellery and other decorative ornaments, and coins.

Platinum is a white metal which was discovered in the silver mines of Mexico. At first no one thought it was very useful because it was difficult to melt. Today it is used to make jewellery. The fact that it is difficult to melt has also made it important to industry. For example, it is used for electrical contacts which get very hot. It does not corrode, so platinum alloys or coatings are used to make some delicate pieces of machinery.

    The main use of precious stones is to be cut into gems which are made into jewellery. Gems are highly valued for their beauty, but they do not look very exciting when they first come out of the earth.

Diamonds

Diamonds are crystals which can be found in loose stones near the surface. Picture [19] shows people panning for diamonds in Sierra Leone. Other parts of West Africa have surface diamonds, and they are also found in India and South America. However, diamonds are also found far below the ground. In the deep South African diamond mines, the crystals are embedded in a rock called kimberlite. You can see this rock being mined in picture [20].

    The stones cannot be smelted out of the rock like metals. They have to be cut. A piece of rock containing a diamond is taken to a skilled craftsman called a diamond cutter who chips away at the rock until the precious stone emerges. It is then cut and shaped so that the light shines through it and brings out the beauty of the stone. It is now called a gem, and is ready to be made into a piece of jewellery.

Other precious stones

The other precious stones are emeralds, rubies, sapphires, and opals. They are all hard, and will not chip or scratch. Emeralds are green, and the best ones come from South America. They are the finest clear crystals of a

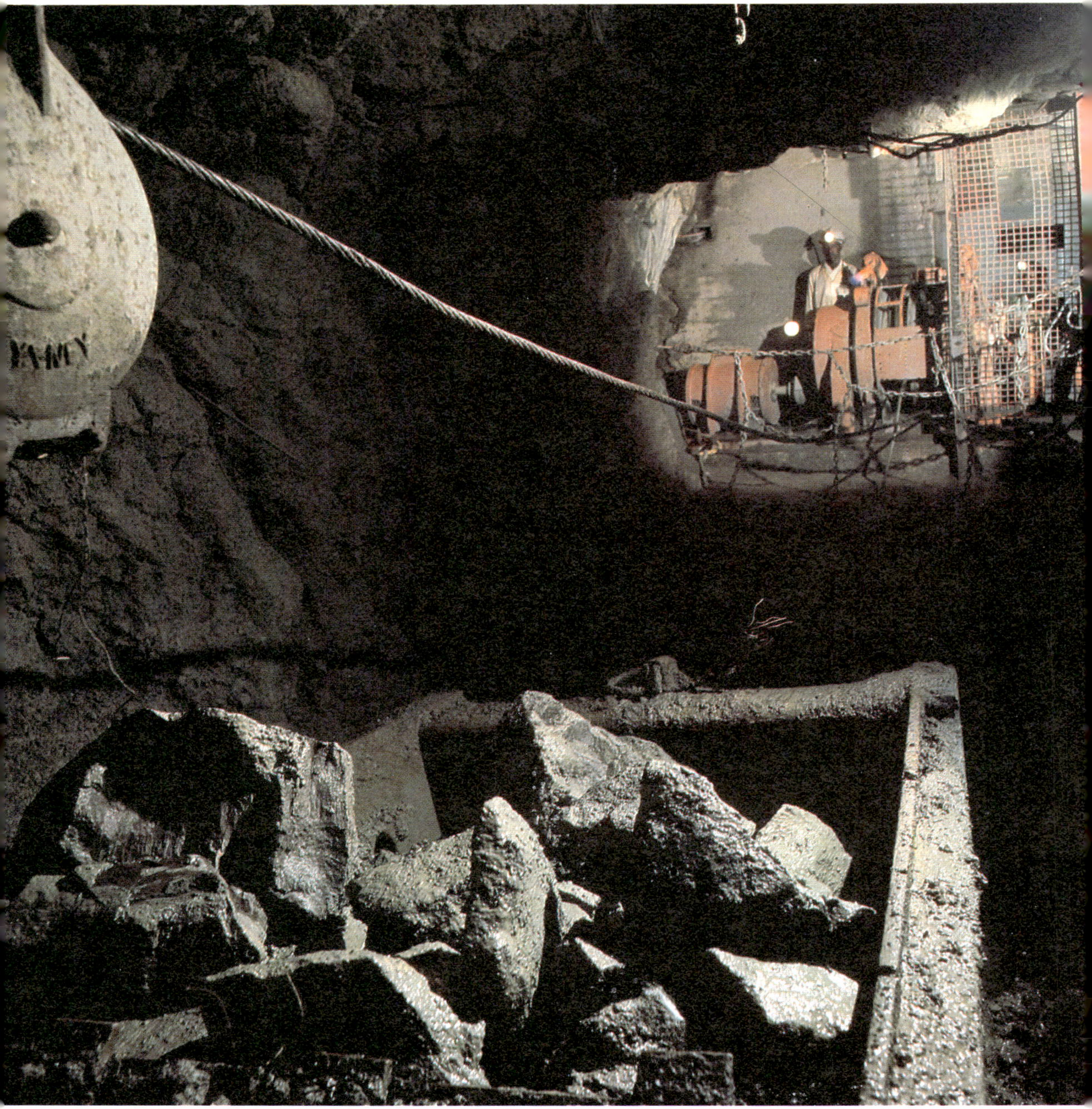

[21]

mineral called beryl.

Rubies are red crystals found in gravels and sedimentary rocks in Burma and Sri Lanka.

Blue sapphires also come from Sri Lanka, and from Australia and the United States.

Opals are found in some sedimentary rocks such as sandstone, and in volcanic rocks. Many of the world's opals come from Australia, like the ones in picture [21]. They may be milky-white, green, yellow, or a fiery red; and they also have other spots of colour when exposed to strong light. Unfortunately, it is impossible for photographs to show the beauty of opals, or any other precious stones.

There are several other beautiful stones which are not so rare and valuable as precious stones. They are called semi-precious.

Precious stones also have industrial uses, because they are so hard. High-speed drills, like those used in oil rigs, have cutters tipped with diamonds. Tiny jewels form part of the mechanism of clockwork watches.

5 · The future for minerals

All the metals and other minerals in this book have one thing in common. They all come from the earth's crust and they took millions of years to form. People have only been on the earth for about 40,000 years, but already our precious store of minerals is in danger of running out.

Picture [22] shows a part of the Antarctic. Diamonds, oil, uranium, coal, and gold have been detected beneath the 2,000-metres deep ice-cap. Scientists from several countries, including the United States, Australia, New Zealand, and Britain are trying to find a way of drilling through the ice to get at them.

Perhaps rocks beneath the sea contain hidden supplies of metals. In the past, people thought it was too expensive and difficult to recover minerals from the sea. However, we

[22]

[23]

now have oil and gas rigs out at sea. Perhaps we can find a way of mining for metals as well.

There is no replacement for metal. We use it in thousands of different ways. We could probably do without diamond rings but what about machine tools, electricity cables, bridges, railway lines, and space satellites.

Look at the scene in picture [23]. Would we have reached the moon without metal spacecraft? And now that we are there, perhaps we will find new metals, with uses we had not even thought of before.

Index

Africa 15
alloys 8, 9, 23
alumina 22
aluminium 9, 15, 22
America 15
amethyst 9
annealing 7
Antarctic 15
aquamarine 9
Australia 15, 22, 26, 30

Bauxite 15, 22
beryl 29
brass 9
Britain 30
bronze 8
Burma 26, 29

Canada 8, 15, 22, 26
carbon 16, 17
cast iron 18, 19
chalk 14
charcoal 17
chromium 19
clay 6, 11
coal 3, 4, 9, 14, 17, 23, 25
coal mines 9, 14
coke 17, 18
copper 4, 6, 7, 8, 9, 14, 15, 17, 23, 25
crystalline rock 12
crystals 12, 27

Darby, Abraham 17
diamonds 3, 4, 9, 12, 14, 24, 27, 29, 30, 31
diamond mines 3, 4, 27
duralumin 23

earthquakes 5

Egypt 7
emeralds 9, 24, 27
Europe 15

gas 31
gems 27
geologists 4, 10, 12, 13
Germany 17
gold 4, 6, 7, 9, 14, 15, 24, 25, 30, 31
gold mines 14, 24
gold plate 24, 25
granite 11, 14
gravel 14, 29

igneous rock 12
India 27
ingots 21
iron 3, 4, 8, 14, 15, 16, 17, 18, 19
iron mines 8
iron ore 16

jewellery 6, 9, 24, 25, 26, 27

kimberlite 27

lead 8, 9, 14, 15, 23
limestone 12
liquid metals 5

magnesium 23
manganese 9
marble 14
mercury 9, 23
Mexico 26
mines, types of
  coal 9, 14
  copper 14
  diamond 3, 14, 27
  drift 14
  gold 14, 24
  iron 8
  opencast 16, 22
  salt 9
  silver 26

Namibia 3
nickel 9, 19
New Zealand 30

oil 30
oil rigs 29, 31
opals 27, 29
opencast mines 16, 22
ores 6
oxygen 19, 22

pewter 9
pig iron 18
platinum 24, 26
precious metals 4, 24
precious stones 4, 9, 24, 29

quaries 14
Quebec 8

Rock, types of
  crystalline 12
  igneous 12
  sedimentary 12, 29
  volcanic 29
rock salt 14
rubies 9, 24, 27, 29

salt 3, 9, 14
sapphires 9, 27
sand 11, 14
sandstone 12, 14, 29
sedimentary rock 12, 29
semi-precious stones 9, 29
Sierra Leone 27
silver 4, 8, 9, 14, 15, 24, 25, 26
silver mines 26
slate 14
smelting 7
South Africa 14, 15, 24, 27
South America 15, 26, 27
Sri Lanka 29
stainless steel 19
steel 4, 14, 16, 17, 18, 19, 20, 21, 22
sulphur 17

tin 8, 9, 19
topaz 9
tungsten 23
Tutankhamun 7

United States 15, 26, 29
uranium 4, 14, 15, 23, 2

volcanoes 5
volcanic rock 29

West Africa 27

zinc 9, 14, 23

Acknowledgements for photographs: Barnaby's Picture Library (John Titchen) 2, (K J Gilbert) 22; British Steel Corporation, title page, 10, 11, 12, 13, 15; Canadian High Commission 4, 16; De Beers, contents page, 1, 6, 19; International Gold Corporation, cover, 3, 8, 17, 18; NASA 23; National Coal Board 7; Pan American World Airways 9; Promotion Australia 21; Shell Photo Service 5; Young Library 14.